E₁

ISBN: 1 84161 215 4

Copyright © Axiom Publishing, 2004.

This edition first published by Ravette Publishing in 2004.

Printed and bound in Malaysia
for Ravette Publishing Limited
Unit 3, Tristar Centre, Star Road, Partridge Green,
West Sussex RH13 8RA
United Kingdom

Em@il Jokes

RAVETTE PUBLISHING

INTRODUCTION

There is nothing better than a good dose of humour to brighten any day. Okay, well, we know food and shelter and health and love and world peace all have their places, but they don't exactly make you laugh in any sidesplitting way. They don't tickle your funny bone like a good joke might. In fact, it would be a pretty strange world without laughter, and everyone would go about with long, serious faces, wondering when someone was going to invent humour. There'd be no, "Why did the chicken cross the road?" or "Did you hear the one about …" The only laughter would be coming from hyenas and God knows what they would find funny!

Have you ever noticed how jokes sent through email somehow seem funnier than normal, garden variety jokes? There are of course, very good reasons for this, but they are technically complicated and although we fully understand them, you won't, so let's just accept that this collection is really funny and you don't care why!

PONDERABLES:

* Why is the time of day with the slowest traffic called rush hour?
* Do you think Houdini ever locked his keys in his car?
* If the #2 pencil is the most popular, why is it still #2?
* When an agnostic dies, does he go to the "great perhaps"?
* If you crossed a chicken with a zebra would you get a four-legged chicken with its own barcode?
* If practise makes perfect, and nobody's perfect, why practise?
* If all the world is a stage, where does the audience sit?
* Is it possible to have deja vu and amnesia at the same time?
* How do you know when it's time to tune your bagpipes?

MISCELLANEOUS THOUGHTS

Early bird gets the worm, but the second mouse gets the cheese—think about this one.

I'm not cheap, but I am on special this week.

I intend to live forever—so far, so good.

If Barbie is so popular, why do you have to buy her friends?

Mental backup in progress—Do Not Disturb!

Support bacteria—they're the only culture some people have.

Ambition is a poor excuse for not having enough sense to be lazy.

Everyone has a photographic memory. Some don't have film.

What happens if you get scared half to death twice?

I used to have an open mind but my brains kept falling out.

How do you tell when you run out of invisible ink?

Laughing stock: cattle with a sense of humour.

Why do psychics have to ask you for your name?

Wear short sleeves! Support your right to bare arms!

OK, so what's the speed of dark?

I tried snorting Coke once, but the ice cubes got stuck in my nose.

* * * * *

THE DATE

A college student picked up his date at her parents home. He'd scraped together every cent he had to take her to a fancy restaurant.

To his dismay, she ordered almost everything expensive on the menu. Appetizers, lobster, champagne...the works. Finally he asked her, "Does your Mother feed you like this at home?"

"No," she said, "but my Mother's not looking to get laid, either."

THE FACTS OF LIFE

The two most common elements in the universe
are hydrogen and stupidity.

If at first you don't succeed, skydiving is not for you.

Money can't buy happiness...
But it sure makes misery easier to live with.

A truly wise man never plays leapfrog with a unicorn.

Always remember to pillage BEFORE you burn.

The trouble with doing something right the first time is
that nobody appreciates how difficult it was.

It may be that your sole purpose in life is
simply to serve as a warning to others.

Law of Probability Dispersal:
Whatever it is that hits the fan will not be evenly
distributed.

* * * * *

RULES

We always hear "the rules" from the female side. Now here are the rules from the male side. These are our rules: Please note ...these are all Numbered "1" ON PURPOSE!

1. Breasts are for looking at and that is why we do it. Don't try to change that.

1. Learn to work the toilet seat. You're a big girl. If it's up, put it down. We need it up, you need it down. You don't hear us complaining about you leaving it down.

1. Saturday = sports. It's like the full moon or the changing of the tides. Let it be.

1. Shopping is NOT a sport. And no, we are never going to think of it that way.

1. Crying is blackmail.

1. Ask for what you want. Let us be clear on this one: Subtle hints do not work! Strong hints do not work! Obvious hints do not work! Just say it!

1. Yes and No are perfectly acceptable answers to almost every question.

1. Come to us with a problem only if you want help solving it. That's what we do. Sympathy is what your girlfriends are for.

1. A headache that lasts for 17 months is a problem. See a doctor.

1. Anything we said 6 months ago is inadmissible in an argument. In fact, all comments become null and void after 7 days.

1. If you think you're fat, you probably are. Don't ask us.

1. If something we said can be interpreted two ways, and one of the ways makes you sad or angry, we meant the other one.

1. You can either ask us to do something or tell us how you want it done. Not both. If you already know best how to do it, just do it yourself.

1. Whenever possible, please say whatever you have to say during commercials.

1. Christopher Columbus did not need directions and neither do we.

1. ALL men see in only 16 colours, like Windows default settings. Peach, for example, is a fruit, not a colour. Pumpkin is also a fruit. We have no idea what Mauve is.

1. If it itches, it will be scratched. We do that.

1. If we ask what is wrong and you say "nothing," we will act like nothing's wrong. We know you are lying, but it is just not worth the hassle.

1. If you ask a question you don't want an answer to, expect an answer you don't want to hear.

1. When we have to go somewhere, absolutely anything you wear is fine. Really.

1. Don't ask us what we're thinking about unless you are prepared to discuss such topics as S.e.x, Sport, S.e.x, Cars or S.e.x.

1. You have enough clothes.

1. You have too many shoes.

1. I am in shape. Round is a shape.

1. Thank you for reading this; Yes, I know, I have to sleep on the couch tonight, but did you know men really don't mind that, it's like camping.

LESSONS ADULTS LEARN FROM KIDS:

There is no such thing as child-proofing your house.

A 4 years-old's voice is louder than 200 adults in a crowded restaurant.

When you hear the toilet flush and the words "Uh-oh" it's already too late.

Super glue is forever.

Garbage bags do not make good parachutes.

Always look in the oven before you turn it on.

Plastic toys do not like ovens.

The spin cycle on the washing machine does not make earth worms dizzy. It will however make cats dizzy.

Cats throw up twice their body weight when dizzy.

Quiet does not necessarily mean don't worry.

A good sense of humour will get you through most problems in life (unfortunately, mostly in retrospect).

TOP 15 REASONS IT'S GREAT TO BE A GUY:

1. A five day vacation requires only one suitcase.
2. All your orgasms are real.
3. You don't have to lug a bag of useless stuff around everywhere you go.
4. You can go to the bathroom without a support group.
5. You can leave a hotel bed unmade.
6. Wedding plans take care of themselves.
7. You don't have to shave below your neck.
8. You can write your name in the snow.
9. Chocolate is just another snack.
10. Flowers fix everything.
11. Three pair of shoes are more than enough.
12. You don't give a rat's ass if someone notices your new haircut.
13. You can sit with your knees apart no matter what you are wearing.
14. Gray hair and wrinkles add character.
15. The remote is yours and yours alone.

If a man says something in the forest, and there is no woman there to hear it, ...is he still wrong?

* * * * *

I love the lines the men use to get us into bed. "Please, I'll only put it in for a minute." What am I, a microwave?
—*Beverly Mickins (American comedienne)*

* * * * *

HOMEWORK:

LeRoy is a 20 year old 9th grader. This is LeRoy's homework assignment. He must use each vocabulary word in a sentence.

* Foreclose — If I pay alimony dis month, I got no money foreclose.

* Rectum — I had two cadillacs, but my ol'lady rectum both.

* Disappointment — My parole officer tol me if I miss disappointment dey gonna send me back to da big house.

* Penis — I be at da doctor and he hand me a cup and say penis.

* Israel — Alonso try da sell me a Rolex. I said, man dat be fake. He said bullshit, dat watch Israel.

* Acoustic — When I be liddle, my uncle bought me acoustic and took me to da pool hall.

* Iraq — When we be at da pool hall, I tol my uncle Iraq, you break.

* Seldom — My cousin gave me two tickets to da Nicks game, so I seldom.

* Odyssey — I tol my brother, you odyssey da tits on dat hoe.

* Income — I be in bed with da hoe and income my wife.

* * * * *

EMOTIONAL NEEDS

Husband and wife are getting all snugly in bed. Their
passion is heating up. Then the wife stops and says: "I
don't feel like it, I just want you to hold me." The
husband says: "WHAT??" The wife explains that he must
not be in tune with her emotional needs as a Woman. The
husband realises that nothing is going to happen and he
might as well deal with it.

So the next day the husband takes her shopping at a big
department. store. He walks around and has her try on
three very expensive outfits. She can't decide. He tells his
wife to take all three of them. Then they go over and get
matching shoes worth $200 each. And then they go to the
Jewellery Department, where she gets a set of diamond
earrings. His wife is so excited. She thinks her husband
has flipped out but she does not care. She goes for the
tennis bracelet. The husband says: "But you don't even
play tennis, but OK if you like it then let's get it." The
wife is jumping up and down so excited she cannot even
believe what is going on. She says: "I am ready to go, lets
go to the cash register."

The husband says: "No — no — no, honey we're not going to buy all this stuff." The wife's face goes blank. "No honey. I just want you to HOLD this stuff for a while." Her face gets really mad and she is about to explode and the Husband says: "You must not be in tune with my financial needs as a Man!!!"

* * * * *

NAMES

If Oprah Winfrey married Deepak Chopra, she'd be Oprah Chopra.

If Olivia Newton-John married Wayne Newton, then divorced him to marry Elton John, she'd be Olivia Newton-John Newton John.

If Woody Allen married Natalie Wood, divorced her and married Gregory Peck, divorced him and married Ben Hur, he'd be Woody Wood Peck Hur.

BUMPER STICKERS:

* Save the whales. Collect the whole set.
* A day without sunshine is like, night.
* On the other hand, you have different fingers.
* I feel like I'm diagonally parked in a parallel universe.
* Honk if you love peace and quiet.
* Despite the cost of living, have you noticed how popular it remains?
* I drive way too fast to worry about cholesterol.
* I intend to live forever - so far so good.
* Bills travel through the mail at twice the speed of cheques.
* The hardness of butter is directly proportional to the softness of the bread.
* Monday is an awful way to spend 1/7th of your life.
* You never really learn to swear until you learn to drive.
* Plan to be spontaneous - tomorrow.

OXYMORONS:

Act naturally	Found missing
Good grief	Almost exactly
Government organisation	Alone together
Sweet sorrow	"Now, then..."
Passive aggression	Clearly misunderstood
Peace force	Plastic glasses
Definite maybe	Pretty ugly
Twelve-ounce pound cake	Diet ice cream
Rap music	Exact estimate

WHO IS JACK SCHITT?
THE LINEAGE IS FINALLY REVEALED

Many people are at a loss for a response when someone says, "You don't know Jack Schitt." Now you can intellectually handle the situation.

Jack is the only son of Awe Schitt and O. Schitt. Awe Schitt, the fertiliser magnate, married O. Schitt, the owner of Needeep N. Schitt Inc. They had one son Jack.

In turn, Jack Schitt, married Noe Schitt, and the deeply religious couple produced 6 children: Holie Schitt, Fulla Schitt, Giva Schitt, Bull Schitt and the twins: Deep Schitt and Dip Schitt.

Against her parent's objections, Deep Schitt married Dumb Schitt, a high school drop out. However, after being married 15 years, Jack and Noe Schitte divorced. Noe Schitt later remarried Ted Sherlock and because her kids were living with them, she wanted to keep her previous name. She was then known as Noe Schitt-Sherlock.

Meanwhile, Dip Schitt married Loda Schitt and they produced a son of nervous disposition, Chicken Schitt.

Two of the other 6 children, Fulla Schitt and Giva Schitt, were inseparable throughout childhood and subsequently married the Happens brothers in a dual ceremony. The wedding announcement in the newspaper announced the Schitt-Happens wedding. The Schitt-Happens children were Dawg, Byrd, and Hoarse.

Bull Schitt, the prodigal son, left home to tour the world. He recently returned from Italy with his new Italian bride, Pisa Schitt.

So now when someone says, "You don't know Jack Schitt", you can correct them.

Family History recorded by Crock O. Schitt.

* * * * *

One good thing about Alzheimer's is you get to meet new people every day.

TECHNOLOGY FOR THE COUNTRY FOLK

What high-tech lingo becomes once it goes to the country:

LOG ON: Making a wood stove hotter.

LOG OFF: Don't add no more wood.

DOWNLOAD: Getting the farwood off the lorry.

MEGA HERTZ: When yer not keerful gettin the farwood

FLOPPY DISC: Whatcha git from tryin to carry too much farwood

SCREEN: Whut to shut when it's blak fly season

BYTE: Whut dem dang flys do

MICRO CHIP: Whut's in the munchie bag

MODEM: Whacha did to the hay fields

KEYBOARD: Whar ya hang the dang keys

SOFTWARE: Them dang plastic forks and knifes

MOUSE: What eats the grain in the barn

MOUSE PAD: That hippie talk fer the rat hole.

GUILT

Howard had felt guilty all day long. No matter how much he tried to forget about it, he couldn't. The guilt and sense of betrayal was overwhelming.

But every once in a while he'd hear that small inner voice trying to reassure him, "Howard. Don't worry about it. You aren't the first doctor to sleep with one of your patients and you won't be the last."

But invariably the other voice would bring him back to reality, "Howard. You're a veterinarian."

* * * * *

FEMINIST'S FAIRYTALE!

Once upon a time, a beautiful, independent, self assured princess happened upon a frog in a pond.

The frog said to the princess, "I was once a handsome prince until an evil witch put a spell on me. One kiss from you and I will turn back into a prince and then we can marry, move into the castle with my mom and you can prepare my meals, clean my clothes, bear my children and forever feel happy doing so."

That night, while the princess dined on frog legs, she kept laughing and saying, "I don't think so."

* * * * *

THINGS TO THINK ABOUT...

* Why doesn't Tarzan have a beard?
* It's a dog eat dog world out there. And they're short on napkins.
* Don't sweat the petty things and don't pet the sweaty things.
* One tequila, two tequila, three tequila, floor.
* Never trust a stockbroker who's married to a travel agent.
* Is boneless chicken considered to be an invertebrate?
* Married people don't live longer than single people. It just seems longer.
* I went to a bookstore and asked the saleswoman, "Where's the self-help section?" She said if she told me, it would defeat the purpose.
* It may be that your sole purpose is to serve as a warning to others.
* Light travels faster than sound. This is why some people appear bright until you hear them speak.
* War doesn't determine who's right, just who's left.
* He who laughs, last...

QUESTIONS: WHY DID THE CHICKEN CROSS THE ROAD?

ANSWERS:

Machiavelli: The point is that the chicken crossed the road. Who cares why? The ends of crossing the road justify whatever motive there was.

Timothy Leary: Because that's the only kind of trip the Establishment would let it take.

The Bible: And God came down from the heavens, and He said unto the chicken, "Thou shalt cross the road." And the Chicken crossed the road, and there was much rejoicing.

Freud: The fact that you thought that the chicken crossed the road reveals your underlying sexual insecurity.

Darwin 1: Chickens, over great periods of time, have been naturally selected in such a way that they are now genetically predisposed to cross roads

Darwin 2: It was the logical next step after coming down from the trees.

Richard M. Nixon: The chicken did not cross the road. I repeat, the chicken did not cross the road.

Jerry Seinfeld: Why does anyone cross a road? I mean, why doesn't anyone ever think to ask, "What the heck was this chicken doing walking around all over the place anyway?"

Martin Luther King, Jr: I envision a world where all chickens will be free to cross roads without having their motives called into question.

Grandpa: In my day, we didn't ask why the chicken crossed the road. Someone told us that the chicken had crossed the road, and that was good enough for us.

Bill Gates: I have just released the new Chicken 2000, which will both cross roads AND balance your cheque book, though when it divides 3 by 2 it gets 1.4999999999.

George Orwell: Because the government had fooled him into thinking that he was crossing the road of his own free will, when he was really only serving their interests.

Colonel Sanders: I missed one?

Pyrrho the Skeptic: What road?

The Sphinx: You tell me.

Buddha: If you ask this question, you deny your own chicken nature.

Ralph Waldo Emerson: It didn't cross the road; it transcended it.

Ernest Hemingway: To die. In the rain.

Saddam Hussein: This was an unprovoked act of rebellion and we were quite justified in dropping 50 tons of nerve gas on it.

Dr. Seuss: Did the chicken cross the road? Did he cross it with a toad? Yes the chicken crossed the road, but why he crossed, I've not been told!

* * * * *

TOP TEN THINGS THAT SOUND DIRTY IN GOLF BUT AREN'T:

1. Nuts...my shaft is bent.

2. After 18 holes I can barely walk.

3. You really whacked the hell out of that sucker.

4. Look at the size of his putter.

5. Keep your head down and spread your legs a bit more.

6. Mind if I join your threesome?

7. Stand with your back turned and drop it.

8. My hands are so sweaty I can't get a good grip.

9. Nice stroke, but your follow through has a lot to be desired.

And the number 1 thing that sounds dirty in golf but isn't:

10. Hold up...I need to wash my balls first.

* * * * *

Creative Ways to Say Someone is Stupid:

* About as sharp as a marble.
* A few clowns short of a circus.
* Not the brightest bulb on the Christmas Tree.
* A few fries short of a Happy Meal.
* I wish I had a blueprint for his brain; I'm trying to build an idiot.
* An experiment in Artificial Stupidity.
* He only has one oar in the water.
* A few beers short of a six-pack.
* Dumber than a box of hair.
* Doesn't have all her Cornflakes in one box.
* The cheese slid off her cracker.
* An intellect rivalled only by garden tools.
* As smart as bait.
* Chimney's clogged.
* Forgot to pay her brain bill.
* His antenna doesn't pick up all the channels.
* Missing a few buttons on his remote control.
* The wheel's spinning, but the hamster's dead.

Fun History Facts to Know and Tell

This is a compilation of actual student bloopers collected by teachers from 8th grade through college.

Ancient Egypt was inhabited by mummies and they all wrote in hydraulics.

They lived in the Sarah Dessert and travelled by Camelot. The climate of the Sarah is such that the inhabitants have to live elsewhere.

The Bible is full of interesting caricatures. In the first book of the Bible, Genesis, Adam and Eve were created from an apple tree. One of their children, Cain, asked, "Am I my brother's son?"

Moses led the Hebrew slaves to the Red Sea, where they made unleavened bread which is bread made without any ingredients.

Solomon had three hundred wives and seven hundred porcupines.

The Greeks were a highly sculptured people, and without them we wouldn't have history. The Greeks also had myths. A myth is a female moth.

Actually, Homer was not written by Homer but by another man of that name.

Socrates was a famous Greek teacher who went around giving people advice. They killed him. Socrates died from an overdose of wedlock. After his death, his career suffered a dramatic decline.

In the Olympic games, Greeks ran races, jumped, hurled the biscuits, and threw the java. Eventually, the Romans conquered the Greeks. History calls people Romans because they never stayed in one place for very long.

Another story was William Tell, who shot an arrow through an apple while standing on his son's head.

Queen Elizabeth was the "Virgin Queen." As a queen she was a success. When she exposed herself before her troops they all shouted, "Hurrah."

It was an age of great inventions and discoveries, Gutenberg invented removable type and the Bible. Another important invention was the circulation of blood. Sir Walter Raleigh is a historical figure because he invented cigarettes and started smoking. And Sir Francis Drake circumcised the world with a 100 foot clipper.

Abraham Lincoln became America's greatest Precedent. Lincoln's mother died in infancy, and he was born in a log cabin which he built with his own hands.

Gravity was invented by Issac Newton. It is chiefly noticeable in the autumn when the apples are falling off the trees.

Johann Bach wrote a great many musical compositions and had a large number of children. In between he practised on an old spinster which he kept up in his attic. Bach died from 1750 to the present. Bach was the most famous composer in the world and so was Handel. Handel was half-German, half-Italian and half-English. He was very large.

Beethoven wrote music even though he was deaf. He was so deaf he wrote loud music. Beethoven expired in 1827 and later died for this.

The sun never set on the British Empire because the British Empire is in the East and the sun sets in the West. Queen Victoria was the longest queen. She sat on a thorn for 63 years. She was a moral woman who practiced virtue. Her death was the final event which ended her reign.

The nineteenth century was a time of a great many thoughts and inventions. People stopped reproducing by hand and started reproducing by machine. The invention of the steamboat caused a network of rivers to spring up. Louis Pasteur discovered a cure for rabbits. Madman Curie discovered radio. And Karl Marx became one of the Marx brothers.

* * * * *

SIGNS OF LIFE...

Maternity Clothes Shop: We are open on labour day.

On Maternity Room Door: "Push,Push,Push."

Optometrist's Office: If you don't see what you're looking for, you've come to the right place.

Muffler Shop: No appointment necessary. We'll hear you coming.

Auto Body Shop: May we have the next dents?

Veterinarians Waiting Room: Be back in 5 minutes. Sit! Stay!

Garbage Truck: We've got what it takes to take what you've got.

Computer Store: "Out for a quick byte"

Restaurant Window: Don't stand there and be hungry, come in and get fed up.

Funeral Home: Drive carefully, we'll wait.

* * * * *

DAILY AFFIRMATIONS

I no longer need to punish, deceive or compromise myself. Unless, of course, I want to stay employed.

A good scapegoat is nearly as welcome as a solution to the problem.

As I let go of my feelings of guilt, I can get in touch with my Inner Sociopath.

I have the power to channel my imagination into ever-soaring levels of suspicion and paranoia.

Today, I will gladly share my experience and advice, for there are no sweeter words than "I told you so."

I need not suffer in silence while I can still moan, whimper and complain.

As I learn the innermost secrets of the people around me, they reward me in many ways to keep me quiet.

I assume full responsibility for my actions, except the ones that are someone else's fault.

As I learn to trust the universe, I no longer need to carry a gun.

Just for today, I will not sit in my living room all day watching TV. Instead I will move my TV into the bedroom.

Who can I blame for my own problems? Give me just a minute... I'll find someone.

I will find humour in my everyday life by looking for people I can laugh at.

I am willing to make the mistakes if someone else is willing to learn from them.

* * * * *

BEST T-SHIRTS OF THE SUMMER

* If They Don't Have Chocolate In Heaven, I Ain't Going.
* I Used To Be Schizophrenic, But We're OK Now.
* Coffee, Chocolate, Men...Some Things Are Just Better Rich.
* Growing Old is Inevitable; Growing Up is Optional.
* If You Want Breakfast In Bed, Sleep In the Kitchen.
* Wanted: Meaningful Overnight Relationship.

WORDS OF WISDOM ...

I can please only one person per day. Today is not your day. Tomorrow's not looking good either.

I love deadlines. I especially love the swooshing sound they make as they go flying by.

Tell me what you need, and I'll tell you how to get along without it.

Accept that some days you're the pigeon, and some days you're the statue.

I don't suffer from stress - I'm a carrier...

Never argue with an idiot. They drag you down to their level then beat you with experience.

* * * * *

If at first you don't succeed, —*redefine success.*

Hard work never killed anyone, —*but why chance it?*

WAYS TO KNOW YOU ARE A WOMAN:

You're a Bitch:

* When asked "Is something bothering you?" reply "NO" then get pissed off when you are believed.

* Become attracted to someone because he is outgoing and loves parties, start dating him and immediately expect him to stop this behaviour.

* Always take an hour longer than promised to prepare for the evening.

* Always hide very important events in very unimportant terms so you can have something to be pissed about when your boyfriend declines because he has pressing business, i.e. You say "It's no big deal, but I was wondering if you would like to visit my parents with me if you are not busy this weekend." when you mean "It means a great deal to me for you to see my family with me this weekend whether or not it is possible!"

* If he pays attention to you, he is smothering you.

* If he gives you space, he is ignoring you.

41

* No matter what the activity, he doesn't do it as well as a past boyfriend.

* If you are trying to sleep, it's because you're exhausted from your almost super-human level of daily achievement, if he is trying to sleep, it's because he is lazy.

* Demand to be treated as an equal in everything ...except when paying for meals, airplane tickets, concerts, drinks, clothes, etc...these are required gifts proving his love.

* * * * *

You have the capacity to learn from your mistakes.
You will learn a lot today.

The Meek shall inherit the earth
...after we're through with it.

HAM AND EGGS:
A day's work for a chicken;
A lifetime commitment for a pig.

Two can live as cheaply as one... *for half as long.*

PROVERBS:

A first grade teacher collected well-known proverbs. She gave each child in her class the first half of a proverb, and had them come up with the rest. Their insight may surprise you...

* Strike While the ...Bug is close.
* It's always darkest before ...Daylight Savings time.
* Don't bite the hand that ...looks dirty.
* A miss is as good as a ...Mr.
* If you lie down with dogs, you'll ...stink in the morning.
* The pen is mightier than the ...pigs.
* An idle mind is ...The best way to relax.
* Where there's smoke there's ...Pollution.
* Happy the bride who ...gets all the presents.
* Two's company, three's ...the Musketeers.
* Laugh and the whole world laughs with you, cry and ...you have to blow your nose.
* If at first you don't succeed ...get new batteries.
* When the blind leadeth the blind ...get out of the way.

THOUGHTS TO GET YOU THROUGH ALMOST ANY CRISIS:

* Indecision is the key to flexibility.
* You cannot tell which way the train went by looking at the track.
* There is absolutely no substitute for a genuine lack of preparation.
* Happiness is merely the remission of pain.
* Nostalgia isn't what it used to be.
* The facts, although interesting, are irrelevant.
* Someone who thinks logically is a nice contrast to the real world.
* I have seen the truth and it makes no sense.
* All things being equal, fat people use more soap.
* Not one shred of evidence supports the notion that life is serious.
* There is always one more imbecile than you counted on.
* This is as bad as it can get, but don't bet on it.
* The trouble with life is, you're halfway through it before you realise it's a 'do-it-yourself' thing.

GOOD MEMORY

There once was a baby elephant and a baby turtle drinking from a river deep in the jungle. For no reason, the turtle reaches over and bites the elephant's tail, really hard.

Years and years later, the same elephant, now grown up, is by the same river, having a drink with his giraffe buddy, when the same turtle that bit him on the tail all those years ago wanders up to the river. The elephant rears back a leg and kicks the turtle as hard as he can, sending him flying way off into the jungle.

"Why did you do that?" the giraffe asks.

"When we both were babies, that turtle bit my tail for no reason," the elephant replied.

"Wow! You must have a good memory!" exclaimed the giraffe.

"Yep!" said the elephant. "I've got Turtle-Recall."

* * * * *

(ACTUAL!) SIGNS:

Sign in London department store:
BARGAIN BASEMENT UPSTAIRS.

In a laundry, on each washing machine:
PLEASE REMOVE ALL YOUR CLOTHES
WHEN THE LIGHT GOES OUT.

In a London office:
AFTER TEA BREAK STAFF SHOULD EMPTY THE
TEAPOT AND STAND UPSIDE DOWN ON THE
DRAINING BOARD.

In a health food shop: CLOSED DUE TO ILLNESS.

In a safari park:
ELEPHANTS PLEASE STAY IN YOUR CAR.

On a repair shop door: WE CAN REPAIR ANYTHING.
(Please knock hard on the door — the bell doesn't work)

In an office building washroom:
TOILET OUT OF ORDER.
PLEASE USE FLOOR BELOW.

JUST JARGON

Assmosis—The process by which some people seem to absorb success and advancement by kissing up to the boss rather than working hard.

Chips and Salsa—Chips = hardware, Salsa = software. "Well, first we gotta figure out if the problem's in your chips or your salsa."

Cobweb Site—A Web Site that hasn't been updated for a long time.

Dead Tree Edition—The paper version of a publication available in both paper and electronic forms.

Dorito Syndrome—Feelings of emptiness and dissatisfaction triggered by living on junk food.

Percussive Maintenance—The fine art of whacking the heck out of an electronic device to get it to work again.

Plug-and-Play—A new hire who doesn't need any training. "The new guy, John, is great. He's totally plug-and-play."

Salmon Day—The experience of spending an entire day swimming upstream only to get screwed in the end.

Seagull Manager — A manager who flies in, makes a lot of noise, shits over everything and then leaves.

Umfriend — A relationship of dubious standing. "This is Hank, my...um...friend..."

World Wide Wait — WWW.

* * * * *

MORE BUMPER STICKERS

* Jesus is coming, everyone look busy.
* Horn broken, watch for finger.
* I'm just driving this way to piss you off.
* Keep honking, I'm reloading.
* Hang up and drive.
* Consciousness: That annoying time between naps.
* Be nice to your kids.
  They'll be choosing your nursing home.
* Ever stop to think, and forget to start again?

TWO NUNS AND A BLIND MAN

Two nuns are ordered to paint a room in the convent, and the last instruction of the Mother Superior is that they must not get even a drop of paint on their habits. After conferring about this for a while, the two nuns decide to lock the door of the room, strip off their habits, and paint in the nude.

In the middle of the project, there comes a knock at the door. "Who is it?", calls one of the nuns. "Blind man," replies a voice from the other side of the door. The two nuns look at each other and shrug, and, deciding that no harm can come from letting a blind man into the room, they open the door. "Nice tits," says the man, "where do you want these blinds?"

* * * * *

Lord, If I can't be skinny, *please let all my friends be fat.*

REAL NEWSPAPER HEADLINES

* Something went wrong in Jet Crash.
* Expert says Police Begin Campaign to Run Down Jaywalkers.
* Drunk Gets Nine Months in Violin Case.
* Is there a Ring of Debris Around Uranus?
* Prostitutes Appeal to Pope.
* Panda Mating Fails; Veterinarian Takes over.
* British left waffles on Falkland Islands.
* Miners Refuse to Work after Death.
* Juvenile Court to Try Shooting Defendant.
* Stolen Painting Found by Tree.
* Two Sisters Reunited After 18 Years in Checkout Line.
* War Dims Hope For Peace.
* If Strike isn't Settled Quickly, It May Last a While.
* Cold Wave Linked to Temperatures.
* Red Tape Holds Up New Bridge.
* Man Struck by Lightning Faces Battery Charge.
* New Study of Obesity Looks for Larger Test Group.
* Astronaut Takes Blame for GAS in spacecraft.
* Kids Make Nutritious Snacks.

THINGS NEVER TO SAY DURING SEX:

Is it in?

You look better in the dark.

Can you finish now? I have a meeting...

Did I tell you, I have herpes?

Hurry up, the games about to start.

By the way, I want to break up.

Is that smell coming from you?

What's your name again?

But you just started!!

Hold on, let me change the channel...

Oh Susan, Susan... I mean Donna... shit.

Just use your finger, its bigger.

Wanna see me take out my glass eye?

I'm out of condoms, can I use a sock?

Don't squirm, you'll spill my beer.

THE NEW PRIEST

A new priest at his first mass was so nervous he could hardly speak. After mass he asked the monsignor how he had done.

The monsignor replied, "When I am worried about getting nervous on the pulpit, I put a glass of vodka next to the water glass. If I start to get nervous, I take a sip."

So next Sunday he took the monsignors advice. At the beginning of the sermon, he got nervous and took a drink. He proceeded to talk up a storm.

Upon his return to his office after mass, he found the following note on the door:

1. Sip the Vodka, don't gulp.
2. There are 10 commandments, not 12.
3. There are 12 disciples, not 10.
4. Jesus was consecrated, not constipated.
5. Jacob wagered his donkey, he did not bet his ass.
6. We do not refer to Jesus Christ as the late J.C.
7. The Father, Son, and Holy Ghost are not referred to as Daddy, Junior and the Spook.

8. David slew Goliath, he did not kick the shit out of him.

9. When David was hit by a rock and knocked off his donkey, don't say he was stoned off his ass.

10. We do not refer to the cross as the "Big T."

11. When Jesus broke the bread at the Last Supper he said, "Take this and eat it for it is my body." He did not say "Eat me."

12. The Virgin Mary is not called "Mary with the Cherry."

13. The recommended grace before a meal is not: Rub-A-Dub-Dub thanks for the grub, yeah God.

14. Next Sunday there will be a taffy pulling contest at St. Peter's, not a peter pulling contest at St. Taffy's.

* * * * *

It's hard to make a comeback
—*when you haven't been anywhere.*

I was only looking at your nametag, —*honest!*

Losing a husband can be hard.
In my case it was almost impossible.

THESE ARE ACTUAL BUMPER STICKERS

* Learn from your parents' mistakes—use birth control.
* We have enough youth, how about a fountain of Smart?
* Lottery: A tax on people who are bad at math.
* It IS as bad as you think, and they ARE out to get you.
* Auntie Em, Hate you. Hate Kansas. Taking the dog
  Dorothy.
* I get enough exercise just pushing my luck.
* All men are idiots, and I married their King.
* Reality is a crutch for people who can't handle drugs.
* I don't suffer from insanity, I enjoy every minute of it.
* Hard work has a future payoff. Laziness pays off NOW.
* Give me ambiguity or give me something else.
* We are born naked, wet, and hungry. Then things get
  worse.
* Always remember you're unique, just like everyone
  else.
* Very funny Scotty, now beam down my clothes.

LIFE WITHOUT CRUTCHES

If you can start the day without caffeine or pep pills.

If you can be cheerful, ignoring aches and pains.

If you can resist complaining and boring people with your troubles.

If you can eat the same food everyday and be grateful for it.

If you can understand when loved ones are too busy to give you time.

If you can overlook when people take things out on you, when through no fault of your own, something goes wrong.

If you can take criticism and blame without resentment.

If you can face the world without lies and deceit.

If you can conquer tension without medical help.

If you can relax without liquor.

If you can sleep without the aid of drugs.

Then, you are almost as good as your dog or your cat.

...AND NOW THEY LAUGH ALL THE WAY TO THE BANK

* "Computers in the future may weigh no more than 1.5 tons." —*Popular Mechanics, forecasting the relentless march of science, 1949.*

* "I think there is a world market for maybe five computers." —*Thomas Watson, chairman of IBM, 1943.*

* "I have travelled the length and breadth of this country and talked with the best people, and I can assure you that data processing is a fad that won't last out the year." —*The editor in charge of business books for Prentice Hall, 1957*

* "But what ... is it good for?" —*Engineer at the Advanced Computing Systems Division of IBM, 1968, commenting on the microchip.*

* "This 'telephone' has too many shortcomings to be seriously considered as a means of communication. The device is inherently of no value to us." —*Western Union internal memo, 1876.*

* "Who the hell wants to hear actors talk?" —*H.M. Warner, Warner Brothers, 1927.*

* "We don't like their sound, and guitar music is on the way out." —*Decca Recording Co. rejecting the Beatles, 1962.*

* "So we went to Atari and said, 'Hey, we've got this amazing thing, even built with some of your parts, and what do you think about funding us? Or we'll give it to you. We just want to do it. Pay our salary, we'll come work for you.' And they said, 'No.' So then we went to Hewlett Packard, and they said, 'Hey, we don't need you. You haven't got through college yet.'" —*Apple Computer Inc. founder Steve Jobs on attempts to get Atari and HP interested in his and Steve Wozniak's personal computer.*

* "Everything that can be invented has been invented." —*Charles H. Duell, Commissioner, U.S. Office of Patents, 1899.*

* "Louis Pasteur's theory of germs is ridiculous fiction."—*Pierre Pachet, Professor of Physiology at Toulouse, 1872.*

* "640K ought to be enough for anybody." —*Bill Gates, 1981.*

BEAUTIFUL BUT BLONDE

On a plane bound for New York the flight attendant approached a blonde sitting in the first class section and requested that she move to coach since she did not have a first class ticket. The blonde replied, "I'm blonde; I'm beautiful; I'm going to New York; and I'm not moving."

Not wanting to argue with a customer, the flight attendant asked the co-pilot to speak with her. He went to talk with the woman, asking her to please move out of the first class section. Again, the blonde replied, "I'm blonde; I'm beautiful; I'm going to New York, and I'm not moving."

The co-pilot returned to the cockpit and asked the captain what he should do. The captain said, "I'm married to a blonde, and I know how to handle this."
He went to the first class section and whispered in the blonde's ear. She immediately jumped up and ran to the coach section mumbling to herself, "Why didn't someone just say so?"

Surprised, the flight attendant and the co-pilot asked what he said to her that finally convinced her to move from her seat. He said, "I told her the first class section wasn't going to New York."

REALLY STUPID PEOPLE

A man in Johannesberg, South Africa, shot his 49-year-old friend in the face, seriously wounding him, while the two practiced shooting beer cans off each other's head.

The Chico, California, City Council enacted a ban on nuclear weapons, setting a $500 fine for anyone detonating one within city limits.

A bus carrying five passengers was hit by a car in St. Louis, but by the time police arrived on the scene, fourteen pedestrians had boarded the bus and had begun to complain of whiplash injuries and back pain.

Police in Radnor, Pennsylvania, interrogated a suspect by placing a metal colander on his head and connecting it with wires to a photocopy machine. The message "He's lying" was placed in the copier, and police pressed the copy button each time they thought the suspect wasn't telling the truth. Believing the "lie detector" was working, the suspect confessed.

When two service station attendants in Ionia, Michigan, refused to hand over the cash to an intoxicated robber, the

man threatened to call the police. They still refused, so
the robber called the police and was arrested.

* * * * *

WHICH CONDOM WOULD YOU USE...?

Nike Condoms: Just do it.

Toyota Condoms: Oh what a feeling.

Pringles Condoms: Once you pop, you can't stop.

Timex Condoms: It takes a licking and keeps on ticking.

KFC Condoms: Finger-Licking Good.

Energizer: It keeps going and going and going....

M&M condom: It melts in your mouth, not in your hands!

The Star Trek Condom: To Boldly Go Where No Man
Has Gone Before.

* * * * *

PROCRASTINATORS CREED:

* I believe that if anything is worth doing, it would have been done already.

* I shall never move quickly, except to avoid more work or to find excuses.

* I firmly believe that tomorrow holds the possibility for new technologies, astounding discoveries, and a reprieve from my obligations.

* I truly believe that all deadlines are unreasonable regardless of the amount of time given.

* If at first I don't succeed, there is always next year.

* I shall always decide not to decide, unless of course I decide to change my mind.

* I know that the work cycle is not plan/start/finish, but is wait/plan/plan.

* I will never put off until tomorrow, what I can forget about forever.

CHURCH BULLETIN BLOOPERS

"Scouts are saving aluminum cans, bottles, and other items to be recycled. Proceeds will be used to cripple children."

"The Ladies Bible Study will be held Thursday morning at 10. All ladies are invited to lunch in the Fellowship Hall after the B.S. is done."

"Low Self-Esteem Support Group will meet Thursday at 7 to 8:30 PM. Please use the back door."

"The Rev. Merriwether spoke briefly, much to the delight of the audience."

"Due to the Rector's illness, Wednesday's healing services will be discontinued until further notice."

"Weight Watchers will meet at 7 PM. Please use large double door at the side entrance."

"Remember in prayer the many who are sick of our church and community."

"The eighth graders will be presenting Shakespeare's Hamlet in the church basement on Friday at 7 PM. The congregation is invited to attend this tragedy."

"Today's Sermon: 'How Much Can a Man Drink?' with hymns from a full choir."

"The outreach committee has enlisted 25 visitors to make calls on people who are not afflicted with any church."

"The choir invites any member of the congregation who enjoys sinning to join the choir."

* * * * *

THE DIFFERENCE BETWEEN DOGS AND CATS

A dog thinks: Hey, these people I live with feed me, love me, provide me with a nice warm, dry house, pet me, and take good care of me... They must be gods!

A cat thinks: Hey, these people I live with feed me, love me, provide me with a nice warm, dry house, pet me, and take good care of me... I must be a god!

USELESS INVENTIONS ...

* A black highlighter pen.

* Glow in the dark sunglasses.

* Battery powered Battery Charger.

* Double sided playing cards.

* Ejector seats for Helicopters.

* Hand powered Chainsaw.

* Solar Powered Flash Light.

* Inflatable Anchor.

* Skinless bananas.

* Inflatable Dartboard.

* Silent Alarm Clock.

* Fireproof Cigarettes.

* Smooth Sandpaper.

* Water-proof towel.

* A book on how to read.

* A dictionary index.

* Non stick Cellotape.

* Powdered water.

* Reusable ice cubes.

* See-through toilet tissue.

* Turnip ice cream.

* * * * *

DOCTOR'S VISIT

A young woman said to her doctor, "You have to help me, I hurt all over."

"What do you mean?" said the doctor.

The woman touched her right knee with her index finger and yelled, "Ow, that hurts." Then she touched her left cheek and again yelled, "Ouch! That hurts, too."

Then she touched her right earlobe. "Ow, even THAT hurts."

The doctor asked the woman, "Are you a natural blonde?"

"Why yes," she said.

"I thought so," said the doctor. "You have a sprained finger."

TOP 10 REASONS WHY BEER IS BETTER THAN RELIGION:

1. No one will kill you for not drinking beer.

2. Beer doesn't tell you how to have sex.

3. Beer has never caused a major war.

4. They don't force beer on minors who can't think for themselves.

5. When you have beer, you don't knock on people's doors trying to give it away.

6. Nobody's ever been burned at the stake, hanged or tortured over their brand of beer.

7. You don't have to wait more than 2,000 years for a second beer.

8. There are laws saying that beer labels can't lie to you.

9. You can prove you have a beer.

10. If you've devoted your life to beer, there are groups to help you stop.

COMPUTER EASE!

The following are new Windows messages that are under consideration:

1. Smash forehead on keyboard to continue.

2. Enter any 11-digit prime number to continue.

3. Press any key to continue or any other key to quit.

4. File not found. Should I fake it? (Y/N)

5. Bad or missing mouse. Spank the cat? (Y/N)

6. Runtime Error 6D at 417A:32CF: Incompetent User.

7. User Error: Replace user.

8. Windows VirusScan 1.0 "Windows found: Remove it? (Y/N)"

9. If you are an artist, you should know that Bill Gates owns you and all your future creations. Doesn't it feel nice to have security?

10. Your hard drive has been scanned and all stolen software titles have been deleted. The police are on their way.

THE WORLD'S BIGGEST LIES...

* The check is in the mail.
* I'll respect you in the morning.
* You get this one, I'll pay next time.
* I never inhaled.
* It's not the money, it's the principle of the thing.
* ...but we can still be good friends.
* She means nothing to me.
* I gave at the office.
* Don't worry, he's never bitten anyone.
* Read my lips: no new taxes.
* I've never done anything like this before.
* Now, I'm going to tell you the truth.
* It's supposed to make that noise.
* ...then take a left. You can't miss it.
* Don't worry, it's OK — I'm sterile.

A BLIND MANS SPORT

A blind man was describing his favourite sport, parachuting.

When asked how this was accomplished, he said that things were all done for him: "I am placed in the door and told when to jump" "My hand is placed on my release ring for me, and out I go."

"But how do you know when you are going to land?" he was asked. "I have a very keen sense of smell and I can smell the trees and grass when I am 300 feet from the ground" he answered.

"But how do you know when to lift your legs for the final arrival on the ground?" he was again asked.

He quickly answered "Oh, the dog's leash goes slack."

YOU KNOW YOU'RE DRINKING TOO MUCH COFFEE
WHEN

You speed walk in your sleep.

You haven't blinked since the last lunar eclipse.

You grind your coffee beans in your mouth.

The only time you're standing still is during an earthquake.

You lick your coffeepot clean.

You spend every vacation visiting "Maxwell House."

You've worn out the handle on your favourite mug.

You go to AA meetings just for the free coffee.

Starbucks owns the mortgage on your house.

Your life's goal IS to "amount to a hill of beans."

Instant coffee takes too long.

You channel surf faster without a remote.

You want to be cremated just so you can spend the rest of eternity in a coffee can.

Your birthday is a national holiday in Brazil.

You name your cats "Cream" and "Sugar."

You have a picture of your coffee mug on your coffee mug.

You can outlast the Energizer bunny.

You soak your dentures in coffee overnight.

Your coffee mug is insured by Lloyds of London.

Your first-aid kit contains two pints of coffee with an I.V. hookup.

* * * * *

Suicidal Twin Kills Sister By Mistake!

Seen it all. Done it all.
Can't remember most of it.

A thing not worth doing isn't worth doing well.

WHAT MEN REALLY MEAN

"Can I help with dinner?"
Really means...
"Why isn't it already on the table?"

"Good idea."
Really means...
"It'll never work. And I'll spend the rest of the day gloating."

"My wife doesn't understand me."
Really means...
"She's heard all my stories before, and is tired of them."

"It would take too long to explain."
Really means...
"I have no idea how it works."

"I'm getting more exercise lately."
Really means...
"The batteries in the remote are dead."

"Take a break, honey, you're working too hard."
Really means...
"I can't hear the game over the vacuum cleaner."

"That's interesting, dear."
Really means...
"Are you still talking?"

"Honey, we don't need material things to prove our love."
Really means...
"I forgot our anniversary again."

"That's women's work."
Really means...
"It's difficult, dirty, and thankless."

"I was just thinking about you, and got you these roses."
Really means...
"The girl selling them on the corner was a real babe."

"I do help around the house."
Really means...
"I once put a dirty towel in the laundry basket."

"I can't find it."
Really means...
"It didn't fall into my outstretched hands, so I'm completely clueless."

"What did I do this time?"
Really means...
"What did you catch me at?"

"You look terrific."
Really means...
"Oh, God, please don't try on one more outfit. I'm starving."

"We share the housework."
Really means...
"I make the messes, she cleans them up."

"I don't need to read the instructions."
Really means...
"I am perfectly capable of screwing it up without printed help."

NEWSPAPER AD

The following is an ad from a real-life newspaper which appeared four days in a row — the last three hopelessly trying to correct the first day's mistake.

MONDAY: *For sale*: R.D. Jones has one sewing machine for sale. Phone 948-0707 after 7 P.M. and ask for Mrs. Kelly who lives with him cheap.

TUESDAY *Notice*: We regret having erred In R.D. Jones' ad yesterday. It should have read "One sewing machine for sale cheap. Phone 948-0707 and ask for Mrs. Kelly, who lives with him after 7 P.M."

WEDNESDAY *Notice*: R.D. Jones has informed us that he has received several annoying telephone calls because of the error we made in the classified ad yesterday. The ad stands corrected as follows: "For sale R.D. Jones has one sewing machine for sale. Cheap. Phone 948-0707 after 7 P.M. and ask for Mrs. Kelly who loves with him."

THURSDAY *Notice*: I, R.D. Jones, have no sewing machine for sale. I smashed it. Don't call 948-0707 as I have had the phone disconnected. I have not been carrying on with Mrs. Kelly. Until yesterday she was my housekeeper but she quit!

ENGLISH LANGUAGE

The European Commission has just announced an agreement whereby English will be the official language of the EU rather than German, which was the other possibility. As part of the negotiations, Her Majesty's Government conceded that English spelling had some room for improvement and has accepted a 5-year phase-in plan that would be known as "EuroEnglish."

In the first year, "s" will replace the soft "c" ...Sertainly, this will make the sivil servants jump with joy. The hard "c" will be dropped in favour of the "k." This should klear up konfusion and keyboards kan have one less letter.

There will be growing publik enthusiasm in the sekond year, when the troublesome "ph" will be replased with the "f." This will make words like "fotograf" 20% shorter.

In the 3rd year, publik akseptanse of the new spelling kan be expekted to reach the stage where more komplikated changes are possible. Governments will enkourage the removal of double letters, which have always ben a deterent to akurate speling. Also, al wil agre that the horible mess of the silent "e's" in the language is disgraseful, and they should go away.

By the 4th yar, peopl wil be reseptiv to steps such as replasing "th" with "z" and the "w" with "v."

During the fifz yar, ze unesesary "o" kan be dropd from vords kontaining "ou" and similar changes vud of kors be aplid to ozer kombinations of leters. After ze fifz yar, ve vil hav a realy sensibl vriten styl. Zer vil be no mor trubls or difikultis and evryvun vil find it easy tu understand each ozer.
ZE DREM VIL FINALI KUM TRU!

* * * * *

Airplane Humour

And, after landing: "Thank you for flying Delta Business Express. We hope you enjoyed giving us the business as much as we enjoyed taking you for a ride."

"There may be 50 ways to leave your lover, but there are only 4 ways out of this airplane..."

LETTER HOME FROM SCHOOL...

Dear Dad,

$chool i$ really great. I am making lot$ of friend$ and $tudying very hard. With all my $tuff, I $imply can't think of anything I need, $o if you would like, you can ju$t $end me a card, a$ I would love to hear from you.

Love, Your $on.

Reply from dad...

Dear Son,

I kNOw that astroNOmy, ecoNOmics, and oceaNOgraphy are eNOugh to keep even an hoNOr student busy. Do NOt forget that the pursuit of kNOwledge is a NOble task, and you can never study eNOugh.

Love, Dad

* * * * *

THE DIFFERENCE BETWEEN MEN AND WOMEN

A man will pay $2 for a $1 item, if he wants it. A woman will pay $1 for a $2 item that she doesn't want because it's on sale.

A woman worries about the future until she gets a husband. A man never worries about the future until he gets a wife.

A successful man is one who makes more money than his wife can spend. A successful woman is one who can find that man.

To be happy with a man you must understand him a lot and love him a little. To be happy with a woman you must love her a lot and don't expect to understand her at all.

Married men live longer than single men, but married men are a lot more willing to die.

Any married man can forget his past mistakes, there's no reason for two people to keep track of the same things.

Men wake up as good looking as when they went to bed., women seem to deteriorate during the night.

A woman marries a man expecting him to change, and he doesn't. A man marries a woman expecting her not to change and she does.

A woman has the last word in any argument. Anything a man says after that is the beginning of a new argument.

* * * * *

NEW COMPUTER VIRUSES

Monica Lewinsky virus ...*Sucks all the memory out of your computer.*

Titanic virus ...*Makes your whole computer go down.*

Disney virus ...*Everything in the computer goes Goofy.*

Mike Tyson virus ...*Quits after one byte.*

Woody Allen virus ...*Bypasses the motherboard and turns on a daughter card.*

Ronald Reagan virus ...*Saves your data, but forgets where it is stored.*

Arnold Schwarzenegger virus ...*Terminates and stays resident. But it will be back.*

RULES AT WORK:

A pat on the back is only a few centimetres from a kick in the butt.

Don't be irreplaceable, if you can't be replaced, you can't be promoted.

The more crap you put up with, the more crap you are going to get.

You can go anywhere you want if you look serious and carry a clipboard.

Eat one live toad the first thing in the morning and nothing worse will happen to you the rest of the day.

If at first you don't succeed, try again. Then quit. No use being a damn fool about it.

Anyone can do any amount of work provided it isn't the work he/she is supposed to be doing.

Important letters that contain no errors will develop errors in the mail.

If you are good, you will be assigned all the work. If you are really good, you will get out of it.

You are always doing something marginal when the boss drops by your desk.

If it wasn't for the last minute, nothing would get done.

When you don't know what to do, walk fast and look worried.

When confronted by a difficult problem you can solve it more easily by reducing it to the question, "How would the Lone Ranger handle this?"

The last person that quit or was fired will be held responsible for everything that goes wrong.

* * * * *

THINGS YOU REALLY DON'T NEED TO KNOW

The average human eats eight spiders in their lifetime at night.

A pig's orgasm lasts for 30 minutes.

If you fart consistently for 6 years and 9 months, enough gas is produced to create the energy of an atomic bomb.

HOW TO MAINTAIN A HEALTHY LEVEL OF INSANITY IN THE WORKPLACE

Page yourself over the intercom. Don't disguise your voice.

Send email to the rest of the company telling them exactly what you're doing. For example: "If anyone needs me, I'll be in the bathroom."

Hi-Lite your shoes. Tell people you haven't lost them as much since you did this.

Every time someone asks you to do something, anything, ask him or her if they want fries with that.

Put your trash can on your desk. Label it "IN."

Feign an unnatural and hysterical fear of staplers.

* * * * *

WEIRD LOCAL USA SEX LAWS

Bozeman, Montana, has a law that bans all sexual activity between members of the opposite sex in the front yard of a home after sundown-if they're nude. (Apparently, if you wear socks, you're safe from the law!)

Clinton, Oklahoma has a law against masturbating while watching two people having sex in a car.

In Connorsville, Wisconsin no man shall shoot off a gun while his female partner is having a sexual orgasm.

A law in Fairbanks, Alaska does not allow moose to have sex on city streets.

In Florida it is illegal for single, divorced, or widowed women to parachute on Sunday afternoons.

In Harrisburg, Pennsylvania it is illegal to have sex with a truck driver inside a toll booth.

In Kingsville, Texas there is a law against two pigs having sex on the city's airport property.

Any couple making out inside a vehicle, and accidentally sounding the horn during their lustful act, may be taken to jail according to a Liberty Corner, New Jersey law.

In Michigan, a woman isn't allowed to cut her own hair without her husband's permission.

An ordinance in Newcastle, Wyoming, specifically bans couples from having sex while standing inside a store's walk-in meat freezer!

In Oblong, Illinois, it's punishable by law to make love while hunting or fishing on your wedding day.

In Oxford, Ohio, it's illegal for a woman to strip off her clothing while standing in front of a man's picture.

A Tremonton, Utah law states that no woman is allowed to have sex with a man while riding in an ambulance.

In Ventura County, California cats and dogs are not allowed to have sex without a permit.

In the state of Washington there is a law against having sex with a virgin under any circumstances. (Including the wedding night).

* * * * *

AT THE OFFICE...

Quote from a recent meeting: "We are going to continue having these meetings, everyday, until I find out why no work is getting done."

A motivational sign at work: "The beatings will continue until morale improves."

A direct quote from the Boss: "We passed over a lot of good people to get the ones we hired."

Quote from the Boss after overriding the decision of a task force he created to find a solution: "I'm sorry if I ever gave you the impression your input would have any effect on my decision for the outcome of this project!"

HR Manager to job candidate "I see you've had no computer training. Although that qualifies you for upper management, it means you're under-qualified for our entry level positions."

Quote from telephone inquiry "We're only hiring one summer intern this year and we won't start interviewing candidates for that position until the Boss' daughter finishes her summer classes.

THE BARBER SHOP

This guy sticks his head into a barber shop and asks, "How long before I can get a haircut?" The barber looks around the shop and says, "About 2 hours." The guy leaves.

A few days later the same guy sticks his head in the door and asks, "How long before I can get a haircut?" The barber looks around at shop full of customers and says, "About 2 hours." The guy leaves.

A week later the same guy sticks his head in the shop and asks, "How long before I can get a haircut?" The barber looks around the shop and says, "About an hour and a half." The guy leaves.

The barber looks over at a friend in the shop and says, "Hey, Bill, follow that guy and see where he goes." In a little while, Bill comes back into the shop laughing hysterically.

The barber asks, "Bill, where did he go when he left here?"

Bill looked up and said, "To your house."

QUESTIONS

1. Do they have a 4th of July in England?

2. How many birthdays does the average man have?

3. Some months have 31 days; how many have 28?

4. A woman gives a beggar 50 cents; the woman is the beggar's sister, but the beggar is not the woman's brother. How come?

5. Why can't a man living in the USA be buried in Canada?

6. How many outs are there in an inning?

7. Is it legal for a man in California to marry his widow's sister? Why?

8. Two men play five games of checkers. Each man wins the same number of games. There are no ties. Explain this.

9. Divide 30 by 1/2 and add 10. What is the answer?

10. A man builds a house rectangular in shape. All sides have southern exposure. A big bear walks by, what colour is the bear? Why?

11. If there are 3 apples and you take away 2, how many do you have?

12. I have two US coins totalling 55 cents. One is not a nickel. What are the coins?

13. If you have only one match and you walked into a room where there was an oil burner, a kerosene lamp, and a wood burning stove, which one would you light first?

14. How far can a dog run into the woods?

15. A doctor gives you three pills telling you to take one every half hour. How long would the pills last?

16. A farmer has 17 sheep, and all but 9 die. How many are left?

17. How many animals of each sex did Moses take on the ark?

18. A clerk in the butcher shop is 5' 10" tall. What does he weigh?

19. How many two cent stamps are there in a dozen?

20. What was the President's name in 1950?

ANSWERS

1. Yes.

2. One.

3. All of them (Twelve).

4. The beggar is her sister.

5. He can't be buried if he isn't dead.

6. Six.

7. No — because he is dead.

8. They aren't playing each other.

9. Seventy.

10. White. The house is at the North Pole so it is a polar bear.

11. Two.

12. Fifty cent piece and a nickel. (The other one is a nickel).

13. The match.

14. Half way. Then he is running out of the woods.

15. One Hour.

16. Nine.

17. None - Noah took them on the ark.

18. Meat.

19. Twelve.

20. Same as it is now.

20 Correct — *Genius.*

17 Correct — *Above Normal.*

15 Correct — *Normal.*

8 Correct — *Nincompoop.*

6 Correct — *Moron.*

3 Correct — *Idiot.*

* * * * *

FIVE REASONS WHY COMPUTERS MUST BE MALE:

1. They're heavily dependent on external tools and equipment.

2. They periodically cut you off right when you think you've established a network connection.

3. They'll usually do what you ask them to do, but they won't do more than they have to and they won't think of it on their own.

4. They're typically obsolete within five years and need to be traded in for a new model. Some users, however, feel they've already invested so much in the damn machine that they're compelled to remain with an under powered system.

5. They get hot when you turn them on, and that's the only time you have their attention.

* * * * *

FIVE REASONS WHY COMPUTERS MUST BE FEMALE:

1. No one but their creator understands their logic.

2. Even the smallest mistakes are immediately committed to memory for future reference.

3. The native language used to communicate with other computers is incomprehensible to everyone else.

4. The message, "Bad command or filename," is about as informative as "If you don't know why I'm mad at you, then I'm certainly not going to tell you."

5. As soon as you make a commitment to one, you find yourself spending half your paycheck on accessories for it.

* * * * *

ACTUAL ANSWERS GIVEN BY CONTESTANTS IN THE
GAME SHOW FAMILY FEUD

Name a song with moon in the title—Blue suede moon.

Name an occupation where you need a torch—A burglar.

Name a famous brother & sister—Bonnie & Clyde.

Something that flies that doesn't have an engine—A
bicycle with wings.

Something associated with the police—Pigs.

A sign of the zodiac—April.

A famous Scotsman—Jock.

Something with a hole in it—Window.

A part of the body beginning with 'N'—Knee.

Something you open other than a door—Your Bowels.

* * * * *

THE THINGS PEOPLE DO

The average cost of rehabilitating a seal after the Exxon Valdez oil spill in Alaska was $80,000. At a special ceremony, two of the most expensively saved animals were released back into the wild amid cheers and applause from onlookers. A minute later they were both eaten by a killer whale.

A psychology student in New York rented out her spare room to a carpenter in order to nag him constantly and study his reactions. After weeks of needling, he snapped and beat her repeatedly with an axe leaving her mentally retarded.

In 1992, Frank Perkins of Los Angeles made an attempt on the world flagpole-sitting record. Suffering from the flu he came down eight hours short of the 400 day record to find that his sponsor had gone bust, his girlfriend had left him and his phone and electricity had been cut off.

A woman came home to find her husband in the kitchen, shaking frantically with what looked like a wire running from his waist towards the electric skillet. Intending to jolt him away from the deadly current she whacked him with a handy plank of wood by the back door, breaking his arm in two places. Until that moment he had been happily listening to his Walkman.

Iraqi terrorist, Khay Rahnajet, didn't pay enough postage on a letter bomb. It came back with "return to sender" stamped on it. Forgetting it was the bomb, he opened it and was blown to bits.

* * * * *

PERFORMANCE APPRAISAL TERMS
...AND THEIR REAL MEANINGS

AVERAGE EMPLOYEE —Not too bright.
EXCEPTIONALLY WELL QUALIFIED — Made no major blunders yet.
CHARACTER ABOVE REPROACH —Still one step ahead of the law.
QUICK THINKING —Offers plausible excuses for mistakes.
CAREFUL THINKER —Won't make a decision.

TAKES PRIDE IN WORK —Conceited.

FORCEFUL —Argumentative.

AGGRESSIVE —Obnoxious.

USES LOGIC ON DIFFICULT JOBS —Gets someone else to do it.

A KEEN ANALYST —Thoroughly confused.

EXPRESSES THEMSELVES WELL —Speaks English.

HAS LEADERSHIP QUALITIES —Is tall or has a loud voice.

EXCEPTIONALLY GOOD JUDGEMENT —Lucky.

CAREER MINDED —Back Stabber.

COMING ALONG WELL —About to be let go.

OF GREAT VALUE TO THE ORGANISATION —Gets to work on time.

EXPERIENCED PROBLEM SOLVER —Screws up often.

INDEPENDENT WORKER —Nobody knows what he/she does.

FORWARD THINKING —Procrastinator.

GREAT PRESENTATION SKILLS —Able to b.s.

GOOD COMMUNICATION SKILLS — Spends lots of time on phone.

LOYAL — Can't get a job anywhere else.

A WOMAN'S RANDOM THOUGHTS

Skinny people piss me off! Especially when they say things like, "You know, sometimes I forget to eat." Now I've forgotten my address, my mother's maiden name, and my keys. But I've never forgotten to eat. You have to be a special kind of stupid to forget to eat.

A friend of mine confused her valium with her birth control pills. She had 14 kids, but she doesn't give a damn.

They keep telling us to get in touch with our bodies. Mine isn't all that communicative but I heard from it the other day after I said, "Body, how'd you like to go to the six o'clock class in vigorous toning?" Clear as a bell, my body said, "listen bitch... do it and die."

I read this article that said the typical symptoms of stress are eating too much, smoking too much, impulse buying and driving too fast. Are they kidding? That is my idea of a perfect day.

REAL ANSWERS TO DRIVING SCHOOL QUESTIONS...

Q. Do you yield when a blind pedestrian is crossing the road?

A. What for? He can't see my license plate.

Q. Who has the right of way when four cars approach a four-way stop at the same time?

A. The pick up truck with the gun rack and the bumper sticker saying, "Guns don't kill people. I do."

Q. What are the important safety tips to remember when backing your car?

A. Always wear a condom.

Q. What changes would occur in your lifestyle if you could no longer drive lawfully?

A. I would be forced to drive unlawfully.

Q. What is the difference between a flashing red traffic light and a flashing yellow traffic light?

A. The colour.

CLASSIC QUOTES

I just broke up with someone and the last thing she said to me was, You'll never find anyone like me again. I'm thinking, I should hope not. If I don't want you, why would I want someone like you?

— Larry Miller

A woman broke up with me and sent me pictures of her and her new boyfriend in bed together. Solution? I sent them to her dad.

— Christopher Case

Relationships are hard. It's like a full-time job, and we should treat it like one. If your boyfriend or girlfriend wants to leave you, they should give you two weeks notice. There should be severance pay, and before they leave you, they should have to find you a temp.

— Bob Ettinger

A lady came up to me on the street and pointed at my suede jacket. 'You know a cow was murdered for that jacket?' she sneered. I replied in a psychotic tone, 'I didn't know there were any witnesses. Now I'll have to kill you too.'

— Jake Johansen

Thou shall not kill. Thou shall not commit adultery. Don't eat pork. I'm sorry, what was that last one? Don't eat pork? God has spoken. Is that the word of God or is that pigs trying to outsmart everybody?

— Jon Stewart

Ever wonder if illiterate people get the full effect of alphabet soup?

— John Mendoza

When I was a kid, I had two friends, and they were imaginary and they would only play with each other.

— Rita Rudner

HOW IT HAPPENS...

In the beginning was the Plan.

And then came the Assumptions.

And the Assumptions were without form.

And the Plan was without substance.

And darkness was upon the face of the Workers.

And the workers spoke among themselves, saying, "This is a crock of shit, and it stinks."

And the Workers went unto their Supervisors and said, "It is a pail of dung, and we can't live with the smell."

And the Supervisors went unto their Managers, saying, "It is a container of excrement, and it is very strong, such that none may abide by it."

And the Managers went unto their Directors, saying, "It is a vessel of fertiliser, and none may abide its strength."

And the Directors spoke among themselves, saying to one another, "It contains that which aids plant growth, and it is very strong."

And the Directors went to the Vice Presidents, saying unto them, "It promotes growth, and it is very powerful.."

And the Vice Presidents went to the President, saying

unto him, "This new plan will actively promote the
growth and vigour of the company with very powerful
effects."

And the President looked upon the Plan and saw that it
was good.

And the Plan became Policy.

And that, my friends, is how shit happens.

* * * * *

SOME BLONDE JOKES...

What did the blonde name her pet zebra?
Spot.

Why do blondes hate M&Ms?
They're too hard to peel.

How can you tell if a blonde's been using the computer?
There's white-out on the screen.

How can you tell when a FAX had been sent from a
blonde?
There is a stamp on it.

BUSINESS STRATEGIES FOR A DEAD HORSE

The tribal wisdom of the Dakota Indians, passed on from one generation to the next, says that when you discover you are riding a dead horse, the best strategy is to dismount. However, in modern business, because of the heavy investment factors to be taken into consideration, often other strategies have to be tried with dead horses, including the following:

1. Buying a stronger whip.

2. Changing riders.

3. Threatening the horse with termination.

4. Appointing a committee to study the horse.

5. Arranging to visit other sites to see how they ride dead horses.

6. Lowering the standards so that dead horses can be included.

7. Appointing an intervention team to re-animate the dead horse.

8. Creating a training session to increase our riding ability.

9. Re-classifying the dead horse as living-impaired.

10. Change the form so that it reads: "This horse is not dead."

11. Hire outside contractors to ride the dead horse.

12. Harness several dead horses together for increased speed.

13. Donate the dead horse to a recognised charity, thereby deducting its full original cost.

14. Providing additional funding to increase the horse's performance.

15. Do a time management study to see if the lighter riders would improve productivity.

16. Purchase an after-market product to make dead horses run faster.

17. Declare that a dead horse has lower overhead and therefore performs better.

18. Form a quality focus group to find profitable uses for dead horses.

19. Rewrite the expected performance requirements for horses.

20. Say things like, "This is the way we have always ridden this horse."

21. Increasing the standards to ride dead horses.

22. Comparing the state of dead horses in todays environment.

23. Declaring that "No horse is too dead to beat."

24. Do a Cost Analysis study to see if contractors can ride it cheaper.

25. Promote the dead horse to a supervisory position.

26. Apply for a government subsidy to retrain dead horses.

* * * * *

SHORT AND (NOT SO) SWEET

How many honest, intelligent, caring men in the world does it take to do the dishes? "Both of them."

Why don't women blink during foreplay?
"They don't have time."

Why does it take one million sperm to fertilise one egg?
"They won't stop to ask directions."

How does a man show that he is planning for the future?
"He buys two cases of beer."

How many men does it take to change a roll of toilet paper? "We don't know; it has never happened."

Why is it difficult to find men who are sensitive, caring and good looking? "They all already have boyfriends."

What do you call a woman who knows where her husband is every night? "A widow."

How did Pinocchio find out he was made of wood?
"His hand caught fire."

How do you get a man to do sit-ups?
"Put the remote control between his toes"

How are men and parking spots alike?
"Good ones are always taken. Free ones are mostly handicapped or extremely small."

What is the one thing that all men at singles bars have in common? "They're married."

Man says to God: "God, why did you make woman so beautiful?" God says: "So you would love her."

"But God," the man says, "why did you make her so dumb?" God says: "So she would love you."

* * * * *

OUT OF THE MOUTHS OF BABES

A three-year-old went with his dad to see a litter of kittens. On returning home, he breathlessly informed his mother there were two boy kittens and two girl kittens. "How did you know?" his mother asked.
"Daddy picked them up and looked underneath," he replied. "I think it's printed on the bottom."

On the first day of school, the Kindergarten teacher said, "If anyone has to go to the bathroom, hold up two fingers." A little voice from the back of the room asked, "How will that help?"

A father was reading Bible stories to his young son. He read, "The man named Lot was warned to take his wife and flee out of the city, but his wife looked back and was turned to salt." His son asked, "What happened to the flea?"

A four-year-old girl was learning to say the Lord's Prayer. She was reciting it all by herself without help from her mother. She said, "And lead us not into temptation, but deliver us some email. AMEN."

RODNEY DANGERFIELD'S BEST ONE-LINERS

n over, there's nobody home. I went over. Nobody was home.

If it weren't for pick-pockets I'd have no sex life at all.

And we were poor too. Why if I wasn't born a boy.... I'd have nothing to play with.

Its been a rough day. I got up this morning .... put on a shirt and a button fell off. I picked up my briefcase and the handle came off. I'm afraid to go to the bathroom.

My mother never breast fed me. She told me that she only liked me as a friend.

I remember the time I was kidnapped and they sent a piece of my finger to my father. He said he wanted more proof.

* * * * *

QUESTIONS:

If a deaf person swears in sign language, does his mother wash his hands with soap?

Why can't they use the material from the 'little black box' for the entire plane?

Is there another word for synonym?

Isn't it a bit unnerving that doctors call what they do "practice?"

When sign makers go on strike, is anything written on their signs?

Why isn't there mouse-flavoured cat food?

What do you do when you see an endangered animal eating an endangered plant?

Would a fly without wings be called a walk?

If a turtle doesn't have a shell, is he homeless or naked?

Can vegetarians eat animal crackers?

Why do they sterilise the needles for lethal injections?

Why did kamikaze pilots wear helmets?

What was the best thing before sliced bread?

WHY?

How come you press harder on a remote-control when you know the battery is dead?

Why are they called apartments, when they're all stuck together?

Do fish get cramps after eating?

How come abbreviated is such a long word?

Why are there 5 syllables in the word "monosyllabic"?

If it's zero degrees outside today and it's supposed to be twice as cold tomorrow, how cold is it going to be?

How do "Keep off the grass" signs get where they are?

Why do ballet dancers always dance on their toes? Wouldn't it be easier to just hire taller dancers?

Why do scientists call it "re"search when looking for something new?

* * * * *

LITTLE JOHNNY

Teacher: Little Johnny, go to the map and show us North America.
Little Johnny: Here it is!
Teacher: Correct. Now, class, who discovered America?
Class: Little Johnny!

Teacher: How can one person make so many stupid mistakes in one day?
Little Johnny: I get up early.

Teacher: Why are you late?
Little Johnny: Because of the sign.
Teacher: What sign?
Little Johnny: The one that says, "School Ahead, Go Slow. "That's what I did."

Teacher: Johnny, give me a sentence starting with "I".
Little Johnny: I is...
Teacher: No, Little Johnny. Always say "I am."
Little Johnny: All right. "I am the ninth letter of the alphabet."

CONFUCIUS SAYS:

"Man who run in front of car, get tired."

"Man who run behind car, get exhausted."

"Man who drive like hell, bound to get there."

"Passionate kiss like spider's web - soon lead to undoing of fly."

"Man who walk through airport turnstile sideways going to Bangkok."

"Man who scratches ass should not bite fingernails."

"War doesn't determine who's right. War determines who's left."

"Man who fight with wife all day, get no piece at night."

"It takes many nails to build crib, but one screw to fill it."

"Man who lives in glass house should change in basement."

"He who fishes in other man's well often catches crabs."

"Man who eat jellybeans fart in living colour."

"Man who fart in church sit in own pew."

ASK GRANDMA

A little girl was out with her Grandmother when they came across a couple of dogs mating on the sidewalk.

"What are they doing, Grandma?" asked the little girl.

The grandmother was embarrassed, so she said, "The dog on top has hurt his paw, and the one underneath is carrying him to the doctor."

They're just like people, aren't they Grandma?" said the little one.

"How do you mean?" asked the Grandma.

"Offer someone a helping hand," said the little girl, "and they f**k you everytime!"

* * * * *

ACCOUNTANTS

What's the definition of an accountant?
—Someone who solves a problem you didn't know you had in a way you don't understand.

What's an auditor?
—Someone who arrives after the battle and bayonets all the wounded.

There are three kinds of accountants in the world:
—Those who can count and those who can't.

What do accountants suffer from that ordinary people don't?
—Depreciation.

An accountant is having a hard time sleeping and goes to see his doctor. "Doctor, I just can't get to sleep at night." "Have you tried counting sheep?"

"That's the problem — I make a mistake and then spend three hours trying to find it."

NO LUCK FINDING THE RIGHT CAREER...

I used to work in an orange juice factory, until I got canned. Yeah, they put the squeeze on me, said I couldn't concentrate. You know, same old boring rind over and over again.

I used to be a lumberjack, but I just couldn't hack it, so they gave me the axe.

I tried to be a tailor, but I just wasn't suited for it. It was a sew-sew job.

I used to work in a muffler factory, until I got exhausted.

I wanted to be a barber, but I just couldn't cut it.

I used to be a deli worker, but I couldn't cut the mustard.

I used to be a musician, but I wasn't noteworthy.

I used to be a doctor, but I didn't have the patients.

FACTS MOST PEOPLE ARE CONTENT TO LIVE
WITHOUT KNOWING:

A duck's quack doesn't echo, and no one can explain
why.

The only fifteen letter word that can be spelled without
repeating a letter is "uncopyrightable."

111,111,111, x 111,111,111 = 12,345,678,987,654,321.

Clans of long ago that wanted to get rid of their unwanted
people without killing them used to burn their houses
down - hence the expression "to get fired."

"I am." is the shortest complete sentence in the English
language.

The term "the whole nine yards" came not from football
but from W.W.II fighter pilots in the Pacific. When
arming their airplanes on the ground, the .50 calibre
machine gun ammo belts measured exactly twenty seven
feet, before being loaded into the fuselage. If the pilots
fired all their ammo at a target, it got "the whole nine
yards."

The phrase "rule of thumb" is derived from an old English law which stated that you couldn't beat your wife with anything wider than your thumb.

The name Jeep came from the abbreviation used in the army for the "General Purpose" vehicle, G.P.

In Cleveland, Ohio, it's illegal to catch mice without a hunting license.

* * * * *

SARCASTIC REMARKS TO GET YOU THROUGH THE DAY

* And your crybaby whiny opinion would be...?
* Do I look like a people person?
* This isn't an office. It's Hell with fluorescent lighting.
* I started out with nothing and still have most of it left.
* I pretend to work. They pretend to pay me.
* Sarcasm is just one more service we offer.
* If I throw a stick, will you leave?
* Well, this day was a total waste of makeup.
* I'm trying to imagine you with a personality.

Things Dogs Must Try To Remember...

* I will not play tug-of-war with Dad's underwear when he's on the toilet.
* The garbage collector is NOT stealing our stuff.
* I do not need to suddenly stand straight up when I'm lying under the coffee table.
* I must shake the rainwater out of my fur BEFORE entering the house.
* I will not eat the cats' food, either before or after they eat it.
* I will not roll on cow flops, dead seagulls, fish, crabs, etc.
* Kitty box crunchies are not food.
* I will not wake Mommy up by sticking my cold, wet nose up her bottom end.
* I will not chew my human's toothbrush and not tell them.
* When in the car, I will not insist on having the window rolled down when it's raining outside.
* The sofa is not a face towel. Neither are Mom & Dad's laps.
* My head does not belong in the refrigerator.
* I will not bite the officer's hand when he reaches in for Mom's driver's license and car registration.

What is a Dog?

1. Dogs lie around all day, sprawled on the most comfortable piece of furniture in the house.

2. They can hear a package of food opening half a block away, but don't hear you when you're in the same room.

3. They can look dumb and lovable all at the same time.

4. They growl when they are not happy.

5. When you want to play, they don't want to play.

6. When you want to be alone, they want to play.

7. They are great at begging.

8. They will love you forever if you rub their tummies.

9. They leave their toys everywhere.

10. They do disgusting things with their mouths and then try to give you a kiss.

Conclusion: They're tiny men in little fur coats.

AN EMAIL OOPS!

It's wise to remember how easily this wonderful technology can be misused, sometimes unintentionally, with serious consequences.

Consider the case of the Illinois man who left the snow-filled streets of Chicago for a vacation in Florida. His wife was on a business trip and was planning to meet him there the next day. When he reached his hotel, he decided to send his wife a quick email. Unable to find the scrap of paper on which he had written her email address, he did his best to type it in from memory.

Unfortunately, he missed one letter, and his note was directed instead to an elderly preacher's wife, whose husband had passed away only the day before. When the grieving widow checked her email, she took one look at the monitor, let out a piercing scream, and fell to the floor in a dead faint. At the sound, her family rushed into the room and saw this note on the screen:

"Dearest Wife,
Just got checked in. Everything prepared for your arrival tomorrow.
PS. Sure is hot down here."

REFLECTING ON YOUR CHANGING CONCERNS!

Then: Long hair.
Now: Longing for hair.

Then: Keg
Now: EKG.

Then: You're growing pot.
Now: Your growing pot.

Then: Trying to look like Marlon Brando
      or Elizabeth Taylor.
Now: Trying not to look like Marlon Brando
      or Elizabeth Taylor.

Then: Getting out to a new, hip joint.
Now: Getting a new hip joint.

* * * * *

QUAYLE'ISMS:

* "I was recently on a tour of Latin America, and the only regret I have was that I didn't study Latin harder in school so I could converse with those people."

* "If we don't succeed, we run the risk of failure."

* "What a waste it is to lose one's mind. Or not to have a mind is being very wasteful. How true that is."

* "I believe we are on an irreversible trend toward more freedom and democracy —but that could change."

* "I have made good judgements in the Past. I have made good judgements in the Future."

* "The future will be better tomorrow."

* "We're going to have the best-educated American people in the world."

* "A low voter turnout is an indication of fewer people going to the polls."

* "We are ready for any unforeseen event that may or may not occur."

* "Quite frankly, teachers are the only profession that teach our children."

* "We're all capable of mistakes, but I do not care to enlighten you on the mistakes we may or may not have made."

* "It isn't pollution that's harming the environment. It's the impurities in our air and water that are doing it."

* "[It's] time for the human race to enter the solar system."

* * * * *

POEM

My face in the mirror isn't wrinkled or drawn;

My house isn't dirty the cobwebs are gone.

My garden looks lovely and so does my lawn;

I think I might never put my glasses back on!

125

HOW TO TALK ABOUT MEN AND STILL BE POLITICALLY CORRECT

He does not have a beer gut,
—He has developed a Liquid Grain Storage Facility.

He is not quiet,
—He is a Conversational Minimalist.

He is not stupid,
— He suffers from Minimal Cranial Development.

He does not get lost all the time,
—He discovers Alternative Destinations.

He is not balding,
— He is in Follicle Regression.

He does not get falling-down drunk,
—He becomes Accidentally Horizontal.

He does not constantly talk about cars,
—He has a Vehicular Addiction.

He is not unsophisticated,
—He is Socially Challenged.

He does not eat like a pig,
—He suffers from Reverse Bulimia.

He is not a male chauvinist pig,
—He has Swine Empathy.

He does not undress you with his eyes,
— He has an Introspective Pornographic Moment.

* * * * *

YOU KNOW YOU'VE BEEN ONLINE TOO LONG WHEN...

* Someone at work tells you a joke and you say "LOL."
* You watch TV with the closed captioning turned on.
* You have called out someone's screen name while making love to your significant other.
* You keep begging your friends to get an account so "we can hang out."
* You begin to say "heh heh heh" instead of laughing.
* You find yourself sneaking away to the computer in the night when your spouse is asleep.

DOG QUOTATIONS

Some days you're the dog; some days you're the hydrant.

—Unknown

Whoever said you can't buy happiness forgot about puppies.

—Gene Hill

A dog teaches a boy fidelity, perseverance, and to turn around three times before lying down.

—Robert Benchley

Don't accept your dog's admiration as conclusive evidence that you are wonderful.

—Ann Landers

No one appreciates the very special genius of your conversation as the dog does.

—Christopher Morley

A dog is the only thing on earth that loves you more than he loves himself.

—Josh Billings

SIGNS THAT YOU'VE HAD TOO MUCH OF THE 21ST CENTURY

* You try to enter your password on the microwave.

* You haven't played solitaire with a real deck of cards in years.

* You have a list of 15 phone numbers to reach your family of 3.

* You email your son in his room to tell him that dinner is ready, and he emails you back "What's for dinner?"

* You chat several times a day with a stranger from South Africa, but you haven't spoken to your next door neighbour yet this year.

* The concept of using real money, instead of credit or debit, to make a purchase is foreign to you.

* Your reason for not staying in touch with family is that they do not have email addresses.

* You consider 2nd day air delivery painfully slow.

* You hear most of your jokes via email instead of in person.

WHY IS A CHRISTMAS TREE BETTER THAN A MAN

* A Christmas tree is always erect.

* Even small ones give satisfaction.

* A Christmas tree stays up for 12 days and nights.

* A Christmas tree always looks good - even with the lights on.

* A Christmas tree is always happy with its size.

* A Christmas tree has cute balls.

* A Christmas tree doesn't get mad if you break one of its balls.

* You can throw a Christmas tree out when it's past its "sell by" date.

* You don't have to put up with a Christmas tree all year.

* * * * *

WHY A CHRISTMAS TREE IS BETTER THAN A WOMAN

* A Christmas tree doesn't care how many other Christmas trees you have had in the past.

* Christmas trees don't get mad if you use exotic electrical devices.

* A Christmas tree doesn't care if you have an artificial one in the closet.

* You can feel a Christmas tree before you take it home.

* A Christmas tree doesn't get mad if you look up underneath it.

* When you are done with a Christmas tree, you can throw it on the curb and have it hauled away.

* A Christmas tree doesn't get jealous around other Christmas trees.

* A Christmas tree doesn't care if you watch football all day.

* A Christmas tree doesn't get mad if you tie it up and throw it in the back of your pickup truck.

QUOTES FROM GROUCHO MARX

"Time flies like an arrow. Fruit flies like a banana."

"Those are my principles. If you don't like them I have others."

"A child of five could understand this. Fetch me a child of five."

"You know I could rent you out as a decoy for duck hunters?"

"You've got the brain of a four-year-old boy, and I'll bet he was glad to get rid of it."

"A man's only as old as the woman he feels."

"I have had a perfectly wonderful evening, but this wasn't it."

"I was married by a judge. I should have asked for a jury."

"I married your mother because I wanted children, imagine my disappointment when you came long."

"Outside of a dog, a book is man's best friend. Inside of a dog, it's too dark to read."

"Quote me as saying I was misquoted."

LIFE LESSONS LEARNED FROM A DOG

* If you stare at someone long enough, eventually you'll get what you want.

* Don't go out without ID.

* Be direct with people; let them know exactly how you feel by piddling on their shoes.

* Be aware of when to hold your tongue, and when to use it.

* Leave room in your schedule for a good nap.

* Always give people a friendly greeting. A cold nose in the crotch is most effective.

* When you do something wrong, always take responsibility (as soon as you're dragged shamefully out from under the bed).

* If it's not wet and sloppy, it's not a real kiss.

* * * * *

KITCHEN WISDOM

* If a messy kitchen is a happy kitchen, this kitchen is delirious.

* No husband has ever been shot while doing the dishes.

* A husband is someone who takes out the trash and gives the impression he just cleaned the whole house.

* If we are what we eat, then I'm easy, fast, and cheap.

* A balanced diet is a cookie in each hand.

* Thou shalt not weigh more than thy refrigerator.

* Blessed are they who can laugh at themselves for they shall never cease to be amused.

* A clean house is a sign of a misspent life.

* Help keep the kitchen clean - eat out.

* Housework done properly can kill you.

* Countless numbers of people have eaten in this kitchen and gone on to lead normal lives.

* My next house will have no kitchen - just vending machines.

THE FOLLOWING QUOTES WERE TAKEN FROM ACTUAL
MEDICAL RECORDS DICTATED BY PHYSICIANS

* Patient has chest pain if she lies on her left side for over
  a year.
* The patient states there is a burning pain in his penis
  which goes to his feet.
* She has had no rigors or shaking chills, but her husband
  states she was very hot in bed last night.
* The patient has been depressed ever since she began
  seeing me in 1983.
* The patient is tearful and crying constantly. She also
  appears to be depressed.
* The patient refused an autopsy.
* The patient has no past history of suicides.
* Patient has left his white blood cells at another hospital.
* Patient was becoming more demented with urinary
  frequency.
* The patient's past medical history has been remarkably
  insignificant with only a 40 pound weight gain in the
  past three days.
* The patient left the hospital feeling much better except
  for her original complaints.

THOUGHTS ON DIETS

* A diet is a weigh of life.

* It's something most of us do religiously: We eat what we want and pray we don't gain weight.

* The problem with curbing our appetites is that most of us do it at the drive in window at McDonalds.

* The most fattening thing you can put in an ice cream sundae is a spoon.

* Diets are for people who are thick and tired of it.

* It's not the minutes spent at the table that put on weight, it's the seconds.

* Most people gain weight by having intimate dinners for two... alone.

* People go to Weight Watchers to learn their 'lessens.'

* A diet is the modern-day meal in which a family counts its calories instead of its blessings.

THE TROUBLED HUMAN RACE

In case you needed further proof that the human race is doomed through stupidity, here are some actual label instructions on consumer goods:

On Sears hairdryer
—Do not use while sleeping.

On Marks & Spencer Bread Pudding
—Product will be hot after heating.

On packaging for a Rowenta iron
—Do not iron clothes on body.

On a Korean kitchen knife
—Warning keep out of children.

On a string of Chinese-made Christmas lights
—For indoor or outdoor use only.

On a Japanese food processor
—Not to be used for the other use.

On Sainsbury's peanuts
—Warning: contains nuts.

On an American Airlines packet of nuts
—Instructions: Open packet, eat nuts.

REASONS WHY ALCOHOL SHOULD BE SERVED AT WORK...

1. It's an incentive to show up.

2. It reduces stress.

3. It leads to more honest communication.

4. It reduces complaints about low pay.

5. It cuts down on time off because you can work with a hangover.

6. Employees tell management what they think, not what management wants to hear.

7. It helps save on heating costs in the winter.

8. It encourages carpooling.

9. Increase job satisfaction because if you have a bad job, you don't care.

10. It eliminates vacations because people would rather come to work.

11. It makes fellow employees look better.

12. It makes the cafeteria food taste better.

13. Salary negotiations are a lot more profitable.

14. Bosses are more likely to hand out raises when they are wasted.

15. Suddenly, burping during a meeting isn't so embarrassing.

16. Employees work later since there's no longer a need to relax at the bar.

17. It makes everyone more open with their ideas.

18. Everyone agrees they work better after they've had a couple of drinks.

19. Eliminates the need for employees to get drunk on their lunch break.

20. Increases the chance of seeing your boss naked.

21. It promotes foreign relations with the former Soviet Union.

22. The janitor's closet will finally have a use.

23. Employees no longer need coffee to sober up.

24. Sitting on the copy machine will no longer be seen as gross.

25. Babbling and mumbling incoherently will be common language.

ENGLISH CAN BE A SILLY LANGUAGE

Lets face it, English is a stupid language.
There is no egg in eggplant.
No ham in hamburger.
And neither pine nor apple in the pineapple.
English muffins were not invented in England

French fries were not invented in France.

We sometimes take English for granted
But if we examine its paradoxes we find that
Quicksand takes you down slowly
Boxing rings are square
And a guinea pig is neither from Guinea nor is it a pig.

If a vegetarian eats vegetables, what the heck does a humanitarian eat!?
You have to marvel at the unique lunacy of a language where a house can burn up as it burns down, and in which you fill in a form by filling it out.

TALKING LIKE A GROWN UP

The former kindergartners were trying to become accustomed to first grade.

The biggest hurdle they faced was that the teacher insisted on no babytalk.

"You need to use 'big people' words" she'd always remind them.

She asked Wendy what she had done over the weekend?

"I went to visit my Nana"

"No, you went to visit your GRANDMOTHER. Use big people words"

She then asked Joey what he had done.

"I took a ride on a choo-choo." he said

"No, you took a ride on a TRAIN, use big people words"

She then asked Eddie what he had done

"I read a book" he replied.

"That's wonderful," the teacher said. "What book did you read?"

Eddie thought about it, then puffed out his chest with great pride and said,....

"Winnie the Sh*t."

HELLO, AND WELCOME TO THE MENTAL HEALTH HOTLINE

If you are obsessive-compulsive, press 1 repeatedly.

If you are co-dependent, please ask someone to press 2 for you.

If you are paranoid, we know who you are and what you want. Stay on the line so we can trace your call.

If you are delusional, press 7 and your call will be transferred to the mother ship.

If you are schizophrenic, listen carefully and a small voice will tell you which number to press.

If you are dyslexic, press 9696969696969.

If you have short-term memory loss, press 9.

If you have short-term memory loss, press 9.

If you have short-term memory loss, press 9.

If you have short-term memory loss, press 9.

If you have low self esteem, please hang up. All our operators are too busy to talk to you.

HONK FOR JESUS

The other day I went to the local religious book store, where I saw a HONK IF YOU LOVE JESUS bumper sticker. I bought it and put it on the back bumper of my car, and I'm really glad I did. What an uplifting experience followed! I was stopped at the light at a busy intersection, just lost in thought about the Lord, and didn't notice that the light had changed. That bumper sticker really worked! I found lots of people who love Jesus. Why, the guy behind me started to honk like crazy. He must REALLY love the Lord because pretty soon, he leaned out his window and yelled, "Jesus Christ!" as loud as he could. It was like a football game with him shouting, "GO JESUS CHRIST, GO!" Everyone else started honking, too, so I leaned out my window and waved and smiled to all of those loving people. There must have been a guy from Florida back there because I could hear him yelling something about a sunny beach, and saw him waving in a funny way with only his middle finger stuck up in the air. I asked my two kids what that meant. They kind of squirmed, looked at each other, giggled and told me that it was the Hawaiian good luck sign. So, I leaned out the window and gave him the good luck sign back. Several cars behind, a very nice black man stepped out of his car and yelled something. I couldn't hear him very well, but it sounded like, "Mother trucker," or "Mother's from there." Maybe he was from Florida, too. He must really love the Lord. A couple of the people were so caught up in the joy of the moment that they got out of their cars and were walking toward me. I bet they wanted to pray, but just then I noticed that the light had changed to yellow, and stepped on the gas. And a good thing I did, because I was the only driver to get across the intersection. I looked back at them standing there. I leaned way out the window, gave them a big smile and held up the Hawaiian good luck sign as I drove away. Praise the Lord for such wonderful folks.

* * * * *